FREE RADICALS AND DISEA

Contents

Foreword

This booklet is about something that is almost certainly going to become common knowledge to the thoughtful and educated citizen of the 21st century. To discuss it in technical detail would be hopelessly confusing, like a non-mathematician trying to understand Einstein's theory of relativity in its mathematical complexity. However, if we reduce this theory to its simplest concept, it teaches us that matter and energy are related. It gives us a foundation by which we can understand the principles involved and use them in a practical way in our daily lives.

This is basically what David Lin has done with the complex subject of "free oxygen radicals." Because of its complexity, it is still a difficult booklet for the average person to read and will require a good attention span. It is not light reading, but, like everything else in our lives, some effort is always required in the process of self-education.

By discussing the role of free radicals in a large number of afflictions, Mr. Lin is making a very important comment that many different diseases are based upon a common cause. This, to a large degree, renders the present, orthodox medical model obsolete. Instead of "making a diagnosis" in clinical terms and then applying a descriptive title, often derived from Latin, we are going to have to face the fact that our diseases have a biochemical origin. Hence, correction of the biochemical abnormality becomes the key factor in addressing the nature of the disease and its treatment.

By a discussion of protective mechanisms, Mr. Lin has clearly pointed to the reason why a whole class of substances are known as antioxidants. Many of them are vital substances which we must obtain from our diet. Thus he places emphasis on the importance of nutrition as a prime source of normal defensive mechanisms. He also points out how free radicals are normal products of energy metabolism, just like sparks are a normal accompaniment of a well-established log fire. Just like the fire must be kept under control, so must free radicals be recognized as a normal effect of metabolism, and also kept under control.

Mr. Lin brings much thought and clinical experience to this booklet. He represents the "new breed" of physicians and reseachers who are intent upon introducing sound and relatively simple answers in dealing with human disease and suffering. The approach that he describes is a great deal more scientific than the present methods of allopathic medicine which are used by the majority of modern physicians. This, like other similar works published by Keats Publishing, deals today with the medicine of tomorrow.

Derrick Lonsdale, M.D.

Introduction

Most of us are aware that certain bacteria, viruses, fungi, and parasites can destroy health if allowed to multiply within us. We also know that the only protection we have is the body's natural defenses: white blood cells, macrophages, antibodies, lymphatic tissue, the thymus gland, and other immune defenses. However, a radically different factor in the battle to maintain health may be involved—excessive amounts of substances called free radicals.

For over 30 years, scientists and medical researchers have substantially increased their knowledge of excessive free radicals and have formulated a theory: Uncontrolled free radical processes may be critically involved in the causation and progression of numerous disease conditions, conditions which before seemed unrelated. Today, research on free radicals is one of the most exciting in nutritional science, perhaps because natural defenses against these harmful substances are very simple nutrients, enzymes, and other natural substances called the antioxidants.

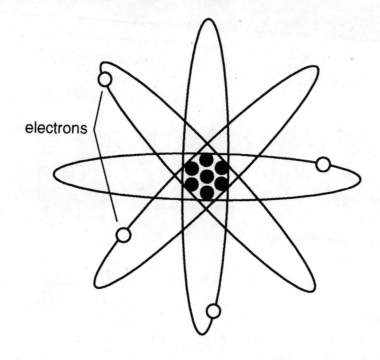

electrons

paired electrons

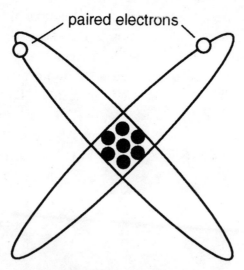

STABLE MOLECULE

Simply described,

free radicals are
molecules
with **electrons** that are **unpaired**.

Molecules are basic building blocks in nature, such as oxygen, fatty acids, amino acids, glucose, and DNA. Molecules are held together by electrons. Stable molecules have electrons that are in pairs, like a buddy system. But if a molecule has an electron that does not have a partner, it becomes unstable and reactive—a free radical. It will steal an electron from a stable molecule.

Once the stable molecule loses an electron, it becomes another free radical. This second free radical will steal an electron from a third molecule, and a destructive cycle begins. Each time a molecule loses an electron, it is damaged and will damage another molecule.

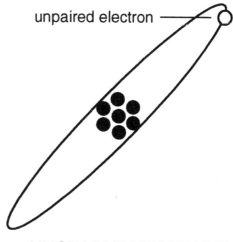

unpaired electron

UNSTABLE MOLECULE

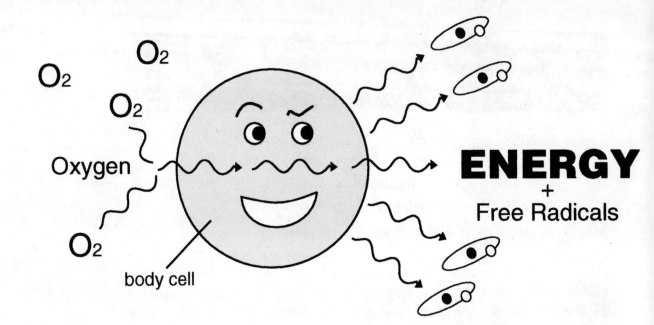

O_2 O_2 O_2 Oxygen O_2 O_2 — body cell — **ENERGY** + Free Radicals

Where Do They Come From?

Free radicals come from three sources—our bodies, the environment, and free radical chain reactions.

Our bodies form free radicals every moment. Living cells need energy to live. This energy comes from reactions involving various substances and oxygen. During this process, intermediates of oxygen are formed, including superoxide and hydroxyl radicals. These intermediates are free radicals. Exercise, illness, and certain medications increase oxygen-related reactions in our bodies, consequently increasing the number of free radicals formed.

Moreover, our immune systems specifically produce free radicals to destroy bacteria and viruses. When we are invaded by harmful microorganisms and our immune systems work overtime, tremendous numbers of free radicals are produced to try to overcome the infection. During these times, controlling the excessive flood of free radicals is vital to protect healthy tissues from damage.

Free radicals are also important in producing vital hormones, or chemical messengers, in the body. Some free radicals activate certain enzymes that produce a wide variety of substances such as prostaglandins, the body's chemical regulators.

Clearly, free radicals are important for health. Without them, we would not be able to produce energy, fight off infectious agents, or produce the chemicals the body needs. Thus, it is very important to understand from the beginning that free radicals are not all bad. Only excessive and uncontrolled amounts of free radicals can damage the body.

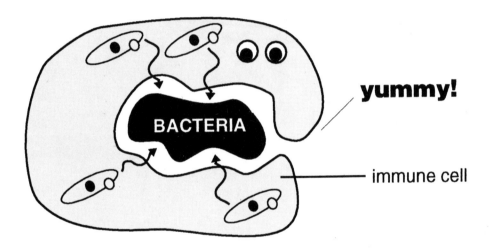

PROCESSES IN OUR BODIES

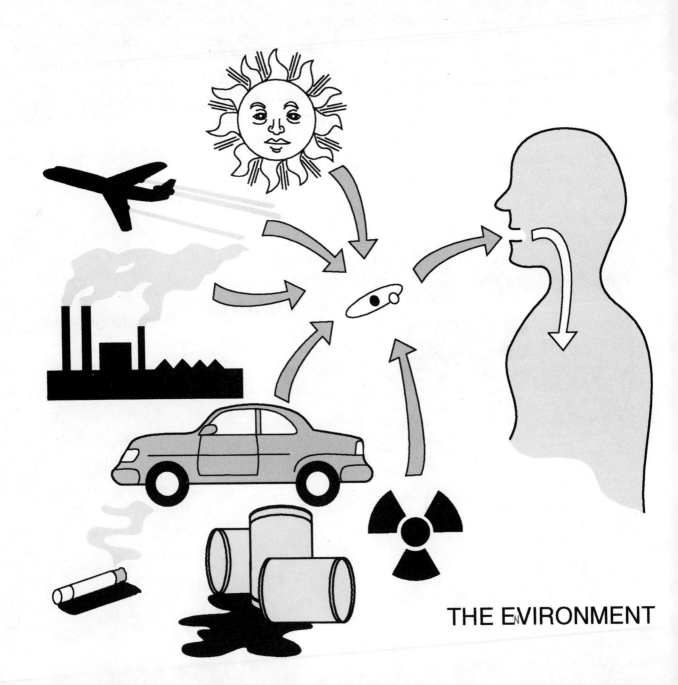

THE ENVIRONMENT

The second source of free radicals is *the environment*. Air pollution, tobacco smoke, excessive radiation, toxic waste and runoff, herbicides, and pesticides all form free radicals, which we inhale or ingest. For instance, ozone is an extremely reactive air pollutant resulting from vehicle exhaust. When we breathe in ozone, it forms free radicals in our lung tissue. Moreover, since blood is constantly being pumped to the lungs for oxygen, ozone-induced free radicals may involve blood cells, diminishing the oxygen supply to the body.

Many of the health woes of the past few decades may be related to the increasing use of dangerous chemicals and technologies, leading to vastly more free radical production than was present a few generations ago. Hopefully, the "green movement" toward cleaning and preserving our environment will result in tremendous reduction of free-radical sources in the environment, substantially decreasing chronic and acute diseases. Earth will treat us well if we treat her well.

Finally, as already described, *free radicals* form other free radicals in chain reactions. One free radical produces a second, which produces a third, and so on. If uncontrolled, cellular damage can result. This domino effect is what makes free radicals so dangerous. Although a free radical regains its electron by stealing it from a stable molecule, it does not regain its original form and function; it is damaged. So, it's not like passing a hot potato for someone else to worry about; it's more like a spreading fire: something that is burned is never the same again. Appendix A provides a more detailed explanation as to how a free radical can initiate a chain reaction.

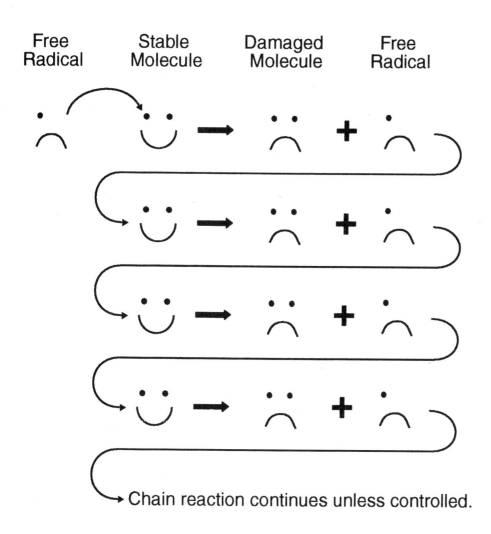

Chain reaction continues unless controlled.

✢ Free Radicals on the Freeway

To picture how free radicals affect us, imagine a car on a highway. Suddenly, one tire rolls over a very big, sharp nail. POW! The tire blows. The car swerves out of control and crashes into another. Vehicles behind cannot stop in time, and the awful crunch of metal echoes for what seems to be forever. One tire blowout has caused great destruction.

The cars represent molecules in our cells, such as proteins, enzymes, fatty acids, and genetic material. The nail is a free radical from reactions in the body or pollution in the environment. The nail damaged the first car by popping its tire. Likewise, a free radical can damage a molecule in our cells by stealing an electron. However, the car with the blowout immediately crashed into another, and a pileup resulted. So, a damaged molecule becomes a free radical, and a chain reaction begins which may implicate many molecules.

We have learned that free radicals can be very dangerous, reactive molecules, since their electrons are unpaired. Formed in the body, the environment, and in self-induced chain reactions, excessive free radicals may cause serious damage to health if uncontrolled. Their highly reactive nature can cause tremendous destruction very quickly, just as an unchecked fire can rapidly burn down an entire city. We will soon discover how rancidity, spoilage, rusting, and burning are all everyday examples of free radicals at work.

Let us first consider specifically how excessive free radicals can damage our cells.

Damage on a Cellular Level

Consider a healthy cell. It has *membrane proteins*, which act as fingerprints of the cell, so that other cells can recognize it. There are *membrane lipids*, arranged in a neat bi-layer, that is, one layer's lipids face out of the cell, and one layer faces in. The membrane lipids are distinct and separate from each other, yet tightly packed in order to form the *cell membrane*, which is the protective coat of the cell. The healthy cell also has a *nuclear membrane*, which sets off the cell's control center, the *nucleus*. Inside the nucleus is housed vital *genetic material*, such as DNA, in nice, neat double helices. And of course, a host of other substances make up the healthy cell.

Free radicals can cause the following devastation:

- Break off the membrane proteins, destroying a cell's identity;

- Fuse together membrane lipids and membrane proteins, hardening the cell membrane and making it brittle;

- Puncture the cell membrane, allowing bacteria and viruses easy entrance;

FREE RADICAL DAMAGE

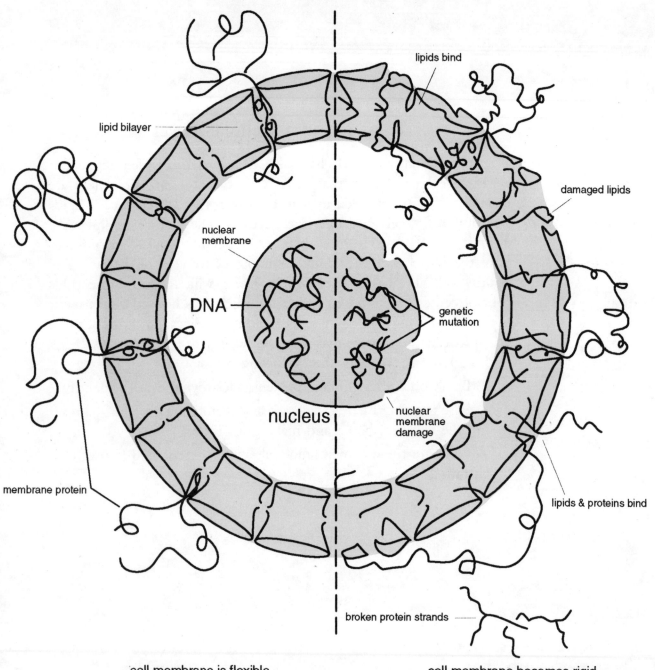

lipids bind

lipid bilayer

damaged lipids

nuclear membrane

DNA

genetic mutation

nucleus

nuclear membrane damage

membrane protein

lipids & proteins bind

broken protein strands

cell membrane is flexible   cell membrane becomes rigid

- Disrupt the nuclear membrane, opening up the nucleus and exposing genetic material;
- Mutate and destroy genetic material, rewriting and destroying genetic information;
- Burden the immune system with the above havoc, plus threaten the immune system itself by undermining immune cells with similar damage.

Appendix B lists common free radicals and the damage they may cause.

This messy picture gets messier, because cellular damage can accumulate to become full-blown disease states. Just as one tiny nail on the freeway can cause a major catastrophe, so a free radical can cause and worsen serious disease conditions, such as . . .

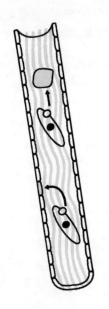

Atherosclerosis

Atherosclerosis is characterized by deposits of plaque on the inside of blood vessels, obstructing normal blood flow.

Research indicates that excessive free radicals may start atherosclerosis by damaging blood vessel cells and lipoproteins. Recall that the cell membrane around a cell is composed of lipids. Lipids are especially susceptible to free radical attack, because electrons are "looser" in lipids than in other types of molecules. For the same reason, lipoproteins, the carriers of cholesterol in the blood, are also very susceptible to free-radical damage. Responding to the damage, immune cells such as macrophages and platelets rush to envelop the affected cells.

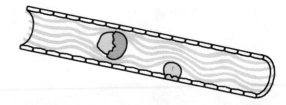

However, these immune cells are "sticky," causing them to attach to the inside of blood vessels. Moreover, other particles in the blood "stick" to them, resulting over time in a massive lump of cells, a plaque. Damaged lipoproteins are also deposited in the plaque, along with the cholesterol they were carrying, which increases the plaque's size and stickiness. Blood flow may thus become seriously compromised, leading to heart attacks, strokes, and high blood pressure.

In spite of its bad reputation, cholesterol itself may *not* be the cause of the heart's problems, but an innocent bystander of free-radical damage. An important distinction exists between normal cholesterol and "oxidized" cholesterol, the latter having been damaged by free radicals. Oxidized cholesterol is concentrated in plaques, and an elevated blood level signifies that the body is losing the battle against free radicals. Normal cholesterol is a vital substance our bodies need to maintain health; it sustains the integrity of every cell and serves as the precursor to many hormones. Only when free radicals damage, or oxidize, cholesterol does its presence increase the risk of heart disease. Thus, limiting dietary intake of cholesterol, though important, should not be the only concern in reducing that risk. Efforts to reduce the presence of excessive free radicals are certainly equally and perhaps more important.

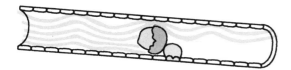
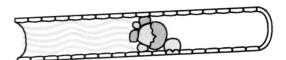

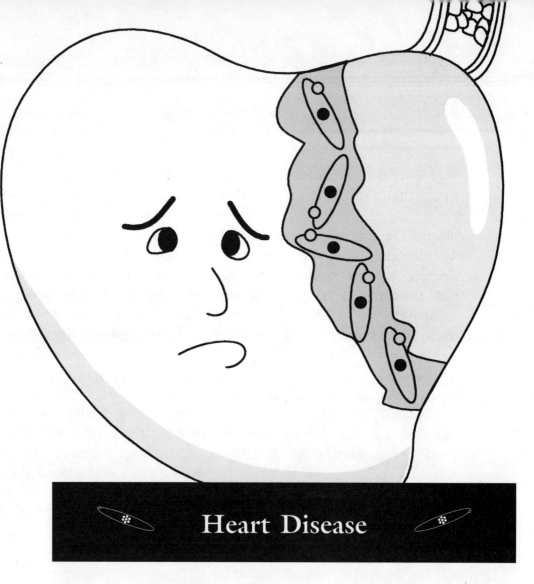

Heart Disease

The heart is the pump which propels life-giving blood to all the body's cells. Just like any other part of the body, the heart needs a constant supply of blood that brings oxygen and nutrients and removes waste. The vessels supplying blood to the heart are known as coronary arteries, and any interruption of this blood supply may lead to certain forms of heart disease and affect the rest of the body.

If uncontrolled free radicals damage cells in the coronary arteries, atherosclerosis may develop and block the normal blood supply to the heart. Heart tissue may then become starved of what it needs to live. Severe pain, or angina pectoris, may result. If not treated, the situation may progress and heart tissue may die. Death of some heart tissue decreases the heart's ability to pump blood, and the whole body suffers. When critical amounts of heart tissue die, the heart may stop pumping altogether, and the person experiences a heart attack, which may be fatal.

Thus, the destructive domino effect of free-radical damage can lead to a heart attack. To make matters worse, free-radical generation is accelerated in dead tissues, because the defenses against them (the antioxidants) no longer function. That is why dead flesh rots so quickly. Indeed, every one of us would quickly grow rancid if our free-radical defenses did not function. In the case of heart disease, the free radicals destroy even more heart tissue, and the heart becomes weaker and weaker.

Cancer

Cancer is the uncontrolled growth and multiplication of cells, resulting in their consuming all available nutrients until healthy cells are starved to death. A cancerous cell is simply a once-normal cell which can't stop growing and multiplying. Researchers believe much of the cause of this erratic behavior lies on a genetic level.

A normal cell contains genes which tell it when to stop growing. If these genes are mutated, such as by free-radical destruction, then the "stop" instruction is lost, and the cell will continue to grow without limitation. The situation is similar to someone removing a stop sign so that cars continue through an intersection without concern or caution (and potential devastation).

Another scenario may be that free radicals turn on a gene, which then overrides any other gene's instruction to stop growing, like someone short-circuiting a traffic light to always be green. Again, the cell receives no instruction to stop growing and will continue devouring available nutrients.

The cancerous cell keeps growing and then multiplies. Now there are two wildly growing cells, which eventually multiply to form four cancer cells, then eight, sixteen, thirty-two, and very quickly, millions and billions. More and more nutrients are demanded by the voracious metabolism of these cells, producing enormous amounts of free radicals, which then destroy surrounding tissues. Soon, not enough nutrients are available and the body starves to death.

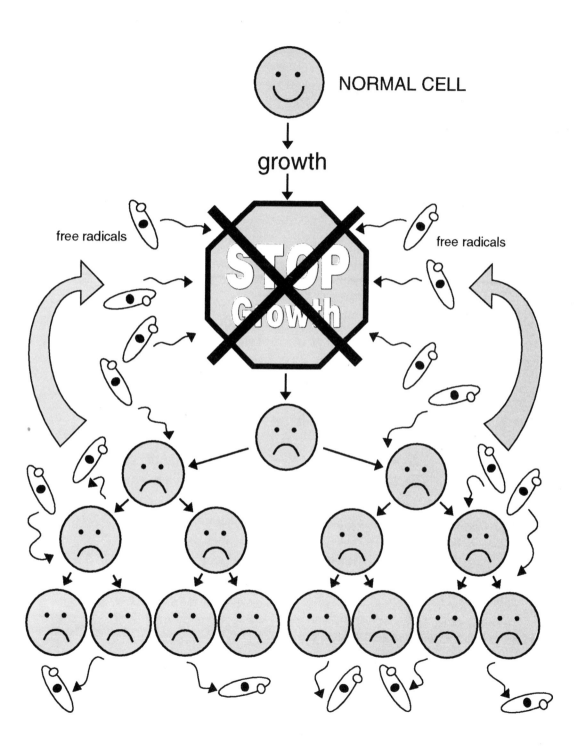

In the early stages of cancer, the immune system tries to contain the proliferating mass by surrounding it with a tough, protective net. Hopefully, the cancer will thus be controlled. However, free radicals can destroy the protective net, allowing the cancerous mass to continue growing.

Ironically, some of the modern treatments for cancer involve using drugs or radiation to destroy cancerous cells by generating huge amounts of free radicals. Unfortunately, this barrage of free radicals will indiscriminately destroy healthy cells as well. As a result, the patient under this treatment may experience profound side effects, such as the loss of hair, weight, energy, immunity, and mental alertness. Some have commented that in certain cases, chemotherapy and radiotherapy may be more deadly to the patient than the original cancer!

Hopefully, with a clearer understanding of how cancer starts and progresses, medical researchers will be able to help cancer patients more effectively. Already, the use of the free radical fighter nutrients, or antioxidants, has been found to alleviate many of the toxic side effects that usually occur during chemotherapy. As is true for most things, prevention is better than cure; antioxidants may help substantially reduce the risk of developing cancer in the first place, as well as other degenerative diseases.

AIDS

AIDS is an acronym for *acquired immunodeficiency syndrome*. The "acquired" represents the observation that AIDS is a disease involving an infectious agent or agents. Whether or not this agent is the human immunodeficiency virus may be debated; however, some agent is involved. The "immunodeficiency" indicates that the human immune system is in some way deficient. In fact, the agent(s) responsible for AIDS apparently attack key immune cells, the helper T-lymphocytes, severely undermining the body's ability to defend itself. Thus, AIDS patients may die from conditions that pose no threat to those with normal immune responses. Finally, the "syndrome" means that AIDS is a condition that includes a set of symptoms which occur together.

Free radicals may play several destructive roles in AIDS. By disrupting cell membranes, they may provide easy entrance for the AIDS virus into helper T-lymphocytes. In other words, those susceptible to the AIDS virus may already have compromised immune systems due to free radicals. There is some evidence that perhaps only 5% to 20% of those infected with the HIV virus actually develop full-blown AIDS, and that another 5% to 20% will not get AIDS itself but AIDS-related conditions; so that a very substantial group of those infected may remain healthy past the expected incubation period of the virus, perhaps indefinitely. This observation strongly suggests the action of mechanisms other than a simple infective agent.

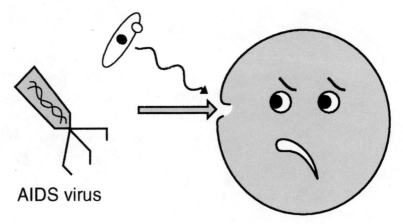

AIDS virus

immune system T or B cell

Perhaps the damaging effects of free radicals play a role in the progression of AIDS. Moreover, by causing damage to the body elsewhere, free radicals may increase the burden on the immune system in general, diminishing the body's ability to effectively combat bacterial and viral invaders.

As with cancer, some modern therapies for AIDS involve drugs which generate free radicals in an effort to kill virally infected cells. Again, severe toxicities may develop, such as an even more diminished immune system. Using antioxidants, the free-radical fighters, along with such therapies has been found to help reduce the toxicities. Moreover, the antioxidants may naturally stimulate the immune system, helping AIDS patients and others suffering from disease to combat bacterial and viral infection from within.

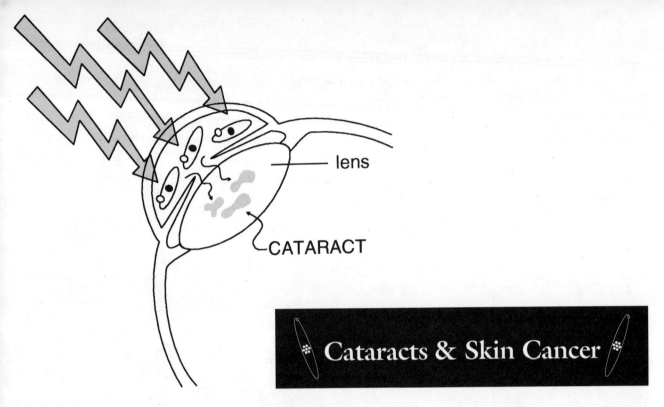

lens

CATARACT

Cataracts & Skin Cancer

Visible light is merely a fraction of the spectrum of radiation that enters our eyes. Ultraviolet radiation also enters our eyes, and due to its high energy, may easily form free radicals in delicate eye tissues. The free radicals may then damage proteins in the lens, causing them to cross-link and precipitate out as solid, opaque masses. These are called cataracts.

Ultraviolet radiation also forms free radicals in the skin. Staying out under the sun too long may burn your skin. Sunburn is the result of massive free-radical damage. In fact, burning by fire involves the same free-radical processes: energized oxygen initiates an uncontrollable cascade of free radicals in once stable material. Sunburn, as well as other burns, may lead to permanent tissue damage.

Constant radiation damage to skin may cause skin proteins to link to each other and/or genetically mutate. Skin cancer may then develop. Because the skin covers such a large area of the body, skin cancer is particularly deadly and difficult to treat. Moreover, skin is the first line of defense against infectious agents, so when it is compromised by cancer, numerous secondary infections may rapidly take hold.

For protection, be sure to wear high-quality sunglasses, which screen out damaging radiation. Likewise, use sunscreen to shield the skin from radiation damage.

Interestingly, eye fluids contain one of the greatest concentrations of free-radical fighters, the antioxidants, in the body. Without these "inner sunglasses," our eyes would rapidly lose their function due to free-radical damage. Researchers have discovered that insufficient levels of antioxidants are associated with greater risks of cataracts. As we shall discover, taking antioxidant supplements may help prevent and treat cataracts, cancer, and other diseases.

HEALTHY JOINT

BONE

JOINT FLUID

BONE

synovial lining

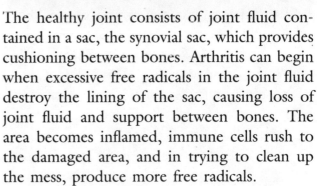

Ar

The healthy joint consists of joint fluid contained in a sac, the synovial sac, which provides cushioning between bones. Arthritis can begin when excessive free radicals in the joint fluid destroy the lining of the sac, causing loss of joint fluid and support between bones. The area becomes inflamed, immune cells rush to the damaged area, and in trying to clean up the mess, produce more free radicals.

Excessive amounts of certain biochemicals cause the inflammation and pain experienced by some arthritic patients. These substances in-

ARTHRITIC JOINT

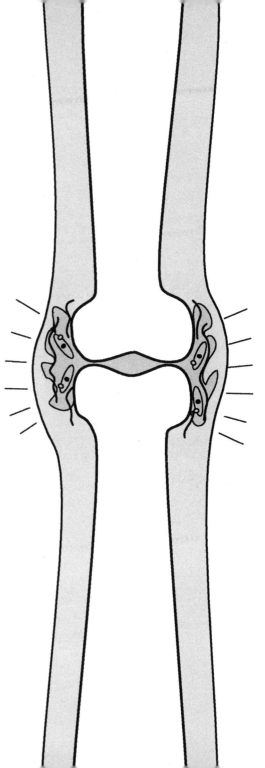

clude prostacyclins and leukotrienes, which are produced from a common fatty acid, arachidonic acid. Beef and other red meats contain high amounts of arachidonic acid, so eating such meats increases arachidonic acid intake which may worsen arthritic conditions.

Antioxidants may inhibit the production of the inflammatory biochemicals from arachidonic acid. Some researchers believe that free-radical damage to cells may cause the excessive production of inflammatory substances, and antioxidants can be useful in correcting the damage.

Aging

The accumulation of free-radical damage may result in aging. Moreover, aging itself may be the result of the diminished ability to control free radicals, which may increase the risk of disease. "Age spots" are actually accumulated pigments which have been damaged by free radicals. Such spots appear not only on the skin but also on organs such as the liver. Some researchers monitor the size and extent of such spots to gauge the extent of aging. Thus, the association between accumulated free-radical damage and aging appears to be very real. Indeed, the elderly seem to be more susceptible to many of the diseases we have discussed.

Recently, scientists discovered an interesting relationship between longevity and factors of aging in humans and other mammals. The levels of free-radical fighters (antioxidants) detected in different mammals were directly related to the species' expected life spans. The higher the levels, the longer they were expected to live. Having the highest levels of antioxidants, humans were found to have the longest life expectancies of all mammals.

Antioxidant supplementation has been shown to effectively boost immune function in the elderly. Can we go a step further and increase life expectancy by controlling free-radical damage? This is certainly an exciting possibility. Having explored how free radicals potentially cause many human diseases, we may reason that efforts to reduce free-radical damage will result in longer, healthier lives. Even if the maximum number of years we can live does not increase, the actual number of years we are alive and healthy may increase.

For instance, studies suggest that the maximum number of years humans can live is 120. Few have approached that age, and the majority become weak and ill much sooner. Perhaps by learning to control excessive free radicals, more of us will not only be able to live to 120 years, but do so in health and strength. In effect, we may be able to almost double our present life expectancy of 70 or so years and make them healthier and more productive.

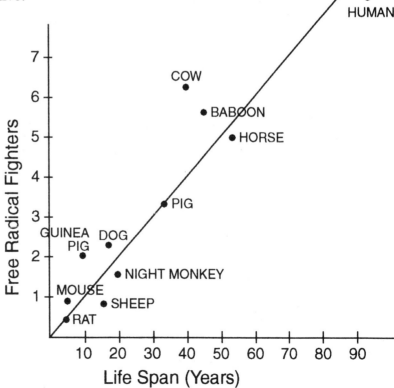

Other Diseases

Researchers are exploring the ways in which free radicals cause and worsen many other disorders, such as Alzheimer's disease, anemia, burns and subsequent infections, complications in surgery, emphysema, hypertension, inflammation, mental disabilities, muscle injury, Parkinson's disease, radiation illness, shock, sterility, and toxicities. The list continues to grow. Moreover, the potential of antioxidant therapies continues to be tested in scientific studies all over the world. The preliminary evidence seems very promising, although much more work needs to be done. A clearer understanding of the processes causing the disorders will hopefully provide the keys to effective treatments, and much of the solution may lie in learning how to control excessive free radicals with antioxidants.

Free-Radical Fighters— the Antioxidants

The free-radical defenses, the antioxidants, have been mentioned many times already. They continually protect us from the destructive actions of free radicals. Let us now focus on the four antioxidant nutrients (beta carotene, vitamin C, vitamin E, and selenium) that are the most promising for medical therapy.

The term "antioxidants" sounds complicated, but is actually easy to understand.

"Anti" means "against," and

"oxidants" are reactive substances that take electrons from other substances, that is, free radicals.

"Oxidant" comes from the word "oxygen." Leave oils and meats outside too long and they become rancid. *Rancidity* involves oxidants in a process called **oxidation**, which is the reaction of oxygen with fatty acids and proteins to form free radicals, eventually causing *spoilage*. *Rusting* is another example of oxidation; oxygen reacts with iron to form a weak, flaky substance, ferrous oxide, or rust. And we have already seen that *burning* is the result of free-radical reactions. So, oxidation, rancidity, spoilage, and burning describe the same thing: free-radical destruction. In fact, knowledge of free radicals began in the 1930s when Leonor Micaelis, chemist at the Rockefeller Institute, puzzled over the reason why oils turn rancid. His discoveries were provocative at the time and spurred tremendous interest in the roles free radicals play in life.

Thus, an antioxidant fights damaging oxidation by neutralizing the free radicals which cause it. Recall that a free radical has an unpaired electron. An antioxidant can supply the missing electron or remove an extra one to stabilize the free radical. The antioxidant then technically becomes a free radical, but thanks to its structure, it is many times less reactive than the original free radical and will not damage other molecules. In terms of free radicals, the buck stops with antioxidants. Further biochemical processes complete the antioxidant process, and a free radical is safely extinguished.

The analogy of the nail on the freeway can also help illustrate how antioxidants function. If a highway sweeper had swept the nail off the road before a car could run over it, then much damage would have been avoided. Or, if the cars had tires protected with impenetrable coatings, then the nail would not be able to puncture them. Antioxidants therefore function as highway sweepers and tire sealants, averting potential devastation.

In the body, many kinds of antioxidants protect us, including enzymes, nutrients, amino acids, proteins, and other biochemicals.

Antioxidant Enzymes

The antioxidant enzymes are synthesized in the body. They initiate processes which ultimately channel the excessive, damaging energies of free radicals into producing harmless substances such as water and ordinary oxygen. These enzymes include

>*glutathione peroxidase,*
>*catalase,* and
>*superoxide dismutase.*

They are produced and function in most cells of the body. In every sense, they are a part of us. Without their protective activity, we would quickly become, quite literally, spoiled. In fact, the reason why dead flesh rots so quickly is that these enzymes no longer function.

The body usually reacts to the presence of increased free radicals by increasing antioxidant enzyme production. For instance, trained athletes usually have higher levels of antioxidant enzymes than most people. Their bodies have adjusted to deal with the extra free radicals from the increased metabolism of strenuous exercise. However, the stress of the modern lifestyle and the toxic by-products of technology have increased the free radical load we all must deal with. Air pollution, industrial waste, pesticide and herbicide residues, and many other sources produce free radicals that did not plague previous generations. Thus, the ability of our bodies to produce sufficient antioxidant enzymes may be stressed and may become insufficient.

Other Antioxidants

Other classes of antioxidant substances exist. Synthetic antioxidants such as dimethyl sulfoxide (DMSO), butylated hydroxyanisole (BHA), and butylated hydroxytoluene (BHT) are used as pharmaceutical agents and food preservatives. Other natural antioxidants include sulfur-containing amino acids and proteins (e.g., cysteine and glutathione), uric acid, and numerous substances derived from herbs.

Antioxidant Nutrients

For human supplementation, most clinical researchers use antioxidant nutrients, because these arc the most practical and cost-effective choices. The antioxidant nutrients most capable of fighting free radicals include

beta carotene (provitamin A),

vitamin C,

vitamin E,

and the mineral *selenium.*

Unlike the enzymes, antioxidant nutrients are not made in the body but are richly supplied in such foods as fruits, vegetables, whole grains, nuts, and seeds. After being absorbed during digestion, they travel in the bloodstream and localize in all the cells and organs to neutralize free radicals. In the process of quenching free radicals, antioxidant nutrients are inactivated, though some may be reactivated, and are eventually eliminated from the body. Thus, they need to be constantly replenished through the diet, just as calories are constantly needed to sustain energy.

The antioxidant nutrients function together as a team to quench free radicals, often in conjunction with other classes of antioxidants, such as the enzymes. One antioxidant does not function in isolation, but each is a part of intricate biochemical chains, like bucket brigades set up to put out fires caused by free radicals. At the same time, each is distinct in chemical structure and nature, and functions in many specialized roles other than that of being an antioxidant. Many books have been written about each one, so the following represents a simplified summary of the main benefits of the antioxidant nutrients.

Beta Carotene (Provitamin A)

Beta carotene can prevent free radical formation and inactivate existing free radicals. It can prevent free radical formation by quenching singlet oxygen—not a free radical itself, but a highly reactive form of oxygen that creates free radicals by transferring excessive energy to stable molecules. Beta carotene is able to absorb and distribute this energy harmlessly through its structure.

Beta carotene is also able to directly neutralize existing free radicals. Researchers are still studying the mechanism by which this free-radical scavenging actually works. As we imagined in our freeway analogy, beta carotene functions as a highway sweeper that brushes a nail (free radical) off the road before it can do damage.

Organic Sunglasses

In the eyes, beta carotene functions like "organic" sunglasses. Actual sunglasses filter out harmful radiation from the sun, which may induce free-radical damage in the eye. Beta carotene is found in high concentration in the eyes and quenches free radicals formed there, preventing pathogenic processes such as cataract formation. Grandma was right: carrots really are good for the eyes! Vitamin C is also important in fighting free radicals in the eyes, and it is no coincidence that the vitamin C concentration of eye fluids is one of the highest in the body.

Beta carotene is also associated with the eyes by being a source of vitamin A. It is actually composed of two vitamin A molecules. When the body is low in vitamin A, special enzymes in the liver are activated and cut the beta carotene in half, releasing two vitamin A molecules. But if vitamin A levels are sufficient, the enzymes remain inactive, and beta carotene remains whole. Thus, beta carotene is considered a safe source of vitamin A, and high doses do not produce the toxic effects associated with excessive levels of vitamin A itself.

SINGLET OXYGEN

Because beta carotene can be stored in the fatty layers under the skin, taking large amounts over time may cause a slight orange-yellow coloration of the skin. In fact, certain "tanning pills" include large amounts of beta carotene specifically for this effect.

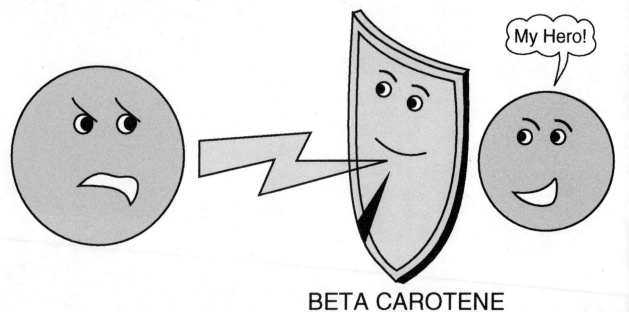

BETA CAROTENE

Reduces Cancer Risk

Beta carotene has been shown in humans to reduce the risk of certain cancers, lung cancer in particular. For this reason, the National Cancer Institute (NCI) and the U.S. Department of Agriculture (USDA) have recommended that individuals increase their consumption of foods rich in beta carotene, such as spinach, kale, carrots, sweet potatoes, winter squash, collards, tomatoes, red peppers, asparagus, broccoli, apricots, and other dark green, orange, or red fruits and vegetables.

Specifically, the NCI and USDA recommend 5.2 to 6.0 mg (8,667 to 10,000 IU) of beta carotene daily. Most Americans get only 1.5 mg (2,500 IU) per day. In other words, most of us need to increase our beta carotene fourfold! For those who never quite grew out of their dislike for vegetables, a supplement would provide a safe, economical means to achieve the recommended levels.

Only 10% to 50% of the beta carotene available from food sources is actually absorbed. Beta carotene is bound in tight complexes in raw foods, which prevents absorption. As little as 1% of the beta carotene in a raw carrot is absorbed by humans. Light cooking helps to release some of the complexes and makes more beta carotene available for absorption. On the other hand, 90% to 100% of beta carotene from nutritional supplements is absorbed. Whether from foods or supplements, beta carotene should be ingested at the same time as other fatty foods to enhance absorption, since it is fat soluble. The presence of fats in the stomach will help stimulate bile and lipase to maximize fat absorption.

Many other carotenes exist, such as alpha, gamma, and delta carotene. Future research may find that these carotenes may be as important to health as beta carotene is.

Vitamin C (Ascorbic Acid)

Vitamin C is another highway sweeper that deactivates free radicals. It works especially in the watery areas of the body, such as blood plasma, lung fluid, eye fluid, and in between cells. Since most of the body (50% to 80%) is composed of water, vitamin C's antioxidant role is especially important.

As a vitamin, ascorbic acid prevents scurvy, a disease in which the vital cellular glue, collagen, disintegrates, resulting in widespread internal bleeding and death. Vitamin C is required to synthesize as well as maintain collagen. Some scientists believe that cancer, atherosclerosis, and other degenerative diseases are actually manifestations of mild scurvy. Vitamin C deficiency comes in degrees, they explain. Approximately 60 mg of vitamin C is needed to prevent scurvy, but that may be insufficient to provide optimal health. Over time, the sub-optimal intake of vitamin C results in mild deficiency, resulting in increasing susceptibility to many diseases.

Recycles Vitamin E

Vitamin C has the unique ability to recycle vitamin E. After vitamin E neutralizes a free radical, it changes into an inactive form that has no antioxidant function. Vitamin C can convert the used vitamin E back to its active antioxidant form, so that it will not be excreted but will continue neutralizing free radicals.

RECYCLES E

70%

Immune Enhancer

Researchers have shown that vitamin C enhances immune function. It can increase white blood cell activity 100% to 300%. It is essential for the production of the antibodies IgA, IgG, and IgM, and the infection-fighting protein C3. Other defenders supported by vitamin C include prostaglandin E_1, B-lymphocytes, T-lymphocytes, and interferon. Moreover, vitamin C can directly destroy certain types of bacteria and viruses. These findings have been used to support the claim that vitamin C prevents and cures colds and flus. Although no clinical study has conclusively demonstrated this, it is important to realize that most researchers have used relatively small dosages of vitamin C in comparison to the amount that is claimed to be optimal; they may not be using enough.

Animals that synthesize their own ascorbic acid produce what would be equivalent to 1000 to 2000 mg in a human being. When such animals encounter stresses, such as injury, illness, or extreme temperatures, their ascorbic acid production increases as much as 100 times normal. Presumably, they require greater vitamin C protection to handle such emergencies. Incidentally, these animals have enzymes that convert glucose, or blood sugar, into ascorbic acid. Humans and a few other animals do not have these enzymes and must obtain ascorbic acid from food.

Most fruits and vegetables are rich in vitamin C. Citrus fruits are almost synonymous with vitamin C. Lemons were used aboard ancient sailing ships to prevent scurvy. Grapefruits, oranges, tomatoes, broccoli, and peppers are other good sources. The inner white, chewy layer of citrus fruits is especially rich in vitamin C, as well as another category of beneficial nutrients, the bioflavonoids.

Vitamin E (Alpha Tocopherol)

Vitamin E is the major lipid-soluble antioxidant nutrient, which means it works in fatty areas, such as the lipids that make up the membrane around every body cell. Just as oils are susceptible to rancidity, so are cell membranes, and hence, so is every cell in the body. Vitamin E can intercalate, or fit in between, the lipid molecules which make up the membrane.

In the analogy of the nail on the highway, vitamin E is like a tough sealant that puncture-proofs the tire so the nail cannot pierce through it. Vitamin E also scavenges free radicals in the blood, joining beta carotene and vitamin C as free-radical highway sweepers.

Moreover, vitamin E is essential to protect us against the ill effects of smog and smoke. For instance, ozone is an air pollutant, produced from nitrogen dioxide, oxygen, and unburned gasoline vapors. Ozone can form free radicals that can affect lung tissue and blood cells.

Helps Reduce Risk of Many Diseases

Vitamin E and other antioxidants have been and are being used clinically in a wide range of diseases. Although more research needs to be done, the evidence we already have shows that the roles vitamin E and other antioxidants play exceed the traditional definition of vitamins. Many scientists are encouraging increased intake of the antioxidants even before conclusive evidence for their benefits has been found.

Increase Vitamin E!

Health professionals encourage us to substitute mono- and polyunsaturated fats for saturated fats, because the latter seem to promote cholesterol production in the body. Polyunsaturated fatty acids are found in light cooking oils (e.g., safflower, sunflower, corn, canola) and fish oils. When you use more of these oils you need to increase vitamin E intake as well. The more unsaturated a fat is, the more it is susceptible to oxidation, and taking large amounts of unsaturated fatty acids without extra vitamin E will quickly use up the body's supply of the vitamin. For instance, one study found that the addition of cod-liver oil to the diet raised the vitamin E requirement about 100-fold. Generally, 1 to 2 IU of extra vitamin E is needed for every gram of polyunsaturated fat consumed.

Foods rich in vitamin E include wheat germ, soybeans, alfalfa, lima beans, sweet potatoes, almonds, pecans, walnuts, peanuts, and other nuts. Nuts and seeds have a high fat content as well, so that increasing consumption of these foods for their vitamin E content will greatly increase the number of calories in the diet. For instance, a diet providing 400 IU from food sources may add several thousand calories to the diet, which will be converted to body fat if not burned off. Thus for vitamin E, supplementation seems more practical and economical to reach the amounts at which beneficial effects are being found. When choosing supplements, you should realize the difference between vitamin E from natural versus synthetic sources.

Natural Superior to Synthetic

Vitamin E is an exception to the rule that natural and synthetic vitamins are identical in form and activity. Natural-source vitamin E (D-alpha tocopherol) consists of only one isomer, while synthetic vitamin E (DL-alpha tocopherol) has eight isomers, only one of which is identical to the one found in nature. Studies show that natural-source vitamin E is significantly more bioactive and bioavailable than its synthetic version.

For instance, 1 mg of D-alpha tocopheryl acetate (natural-source) has a biological activity of 1.36 IU, while the same amount of DL-alpha tocopheryl acetate (synthetic) has a value of only 1.00 IU. Thus, an equal amount of natural-source vitamin E is 36% more bioactive than the synthetic. If the comparison ended there, a simple solution would be to administer more synthetic vitamin E to match the IU activity of natural-source vitamin E. However, further research has revealed that natural-source vitamin E is retained in the body longer than synthetic; it has a longer bioactive life.

These observations have led some researchers to theorize that the seven non-natural isomers in synthetic vitamin E interfere with the one natural isomer. Hence, for maximum antioxidant value, choose products providing vitamin E from completely natural sources. Economically and practically, natural-source vitamin E appears superior.

In relation to other nutrients, vitamin E protects vitamin A from destruction in the body and works together with the mineral selenium.

FREE RADICAL

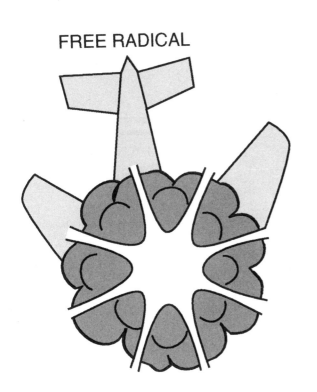

SELENIUM

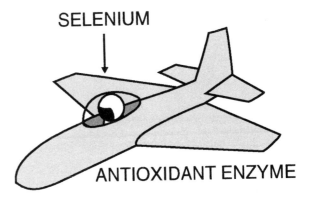

ANTIOXIDANT ENZYME

Selenium

Selenium is one of the ten essential trace minerals. It is a vital component of the enzymes glutathione peroxidase and phospholipid glutathione peroxidase, which neutralize harmful hydrogen peroxide molecules within and between cells. People deficient in selenium exhibit reduced activity of these enzymes. Also, selenium is itself a potent antioxidant and acts in concert with vitamin E, in many cases against the same type of free radicals.

Vital for Health

Supplementation with selenium enhances the immune system, offering protection against cancer. A study in the United States and Canada found that populations living on land that had higher selenium contents of soil and crops experienced fewer deaths from cancer. Numerous animal experiments show that selenium supplementation can significantly reduce cancer risk.

Selenium is also vital in maintaining the elasticity of body tissues, perhaps by helping to prevent oxidation of polyunsaturated fatty acids that help keep tissues supple. A deficiency of selenium has been shown to trigger blood clots, which could initiate heart attacks and strokes. Also, selenium seems to be required to maintain proper muscle mass and tone. Without selenium, the heart collapses into a flat, flaccid sheet of tissue, devoid of fiber and muscle.

Foods rich in selenium include seafood, liver, cashews, peanuts, wheat germ, brown rice, broccoli, barley, bran, and brewer's yeast. Selenium-poor soil, however, produces selenium-poor crops. Animals grazed on soil low in selenium or fed selenium-poor feed also become deficient in the mineral. For instance, cattle and sheep raised in New Zealand, where soils may be low in selenium, have developed muscle degeneration and heart failure. Moreover, the intake of selenium of the general population of New Zealand is much less than that of people in other countries such as the United States. Thus, in choosing foods for selenium, you should consider where they were grown or raised.

The recommended daily requirement of 50-70 mcg of selenium has been established. Notice that this figure is in micrograms, a very tiny amount. One microgram is 1000 times less than one milligram. Thus, selenium is a trace mineral, because it is needed only in trace amounts. The average American diet provides about 50 mcg per day. No one should take more than 1000 mcg of selenium a day, due to the potential for adverse effects.

More Is Not Better

Studies on selenium toxicity (selenosis) have been done mostly on animals. Inorganic salts, such as sodium selenite, appear to be the most potentially toxic in high doses. Only recently have human cases of selenosis from dietary sources been documented in China. The most common symptoms were hair and nail loss. However, these symptoms resulted from selenium intakes far exceeding what is recommended for health. A lot of any good thing may not be better!

Appendix C summarizes the principal roles of the four main antioxidant nutrients.

Review of Current Clinical Uses
of Antioxidants

Let us now consider the latest clinical studies using antioxidant nutrients in treating many kinds of disorders. These studies represent the application and confirmation of theory, and the results are exciting. Hundreds of other studies have been done, are currently in progress, or are being prepared. Major newspapers are giving front-page coverage to the results of some of them. Keep an eye and ear out for the most current news. In terms of nutritional science, today is a very exciting time to be alive.

Antioxidants Reduce Free Radical Levels
in the Blood

Does taking antioxidant vitamins actually reduce free radical levels in the blood? The following study offers impressive substantiation.

One hundred subjects 60 to 100 years of age were separated into three groups. One group was given 200 IU vitamin E daily, another group, 400 mg vitamin C, and the third, both antioxidant vitamins. After four months, significant decreases of free radicals in the blood could be detected:

vitamin E group	14% decrease;
vitamin C group	8% decrease;
both vitamins E & C group	20% decrease.

After 12 months of daily supplementation, the blood free-radical levels decreased even more:

vitamin E group	26% decrease;
vitamin C group	13% decrease;
both vitamins E & C group	25% decrease.

The researchers concluded that supplementation of vitamins E and C, even at small doses, decreased blood free-radical levels in elderly subjects.

Wartanowicz, M., et al. The effect of alpha-tocopherol and ascorbic acid on the serum lipid peroxide level in elderly people. *Annals of Nutrition and Metabolism*. 1984; 28:186-191.

Increasing Antioxidant Protection in Aging

Blood levels of free radicals apparently increase with age. Moreover, the lower the levels of vitamin E and C, the higher the levels of free radicals. In a study, elderly women ages 60 to 100 took 200 IU vitamin E or 400 mg vitamin C for two years. In vitamin E-supplemented subjects, the average free-radical levels in the blood decreased by 20%, while vitamin C-supplemented subjects enjoyed an average decrease of 11%.

The researchers concluded, "The obtained data suggest that vitamin C and vitamin E may beneficially influence some processes of aging."

Ziemlanski, S., et al. The effect of two-year supplementation with ascorbic acid and alpha tocopherol on lipid, hematological and vitamin state in elderly women. *International Metabolism.* 1984; 13:7-14.

Antioxidants Enhance Immunity
in Hospitalized Elderly

Many antioxidant vitamins enhance the immune system to help the body cope with unhealthy invaders. The elderly are particularly susceptible to immune deficiencies, and thus may benefit tremendously by taking antioxidant nutrients.

In a controlled trial, 30 elderly patients who had been hospitalized for several months were randomly separated into two groups. One group received 8000 IU of vitamin A, 100 mg of vitamin C, and 50 mg of vitamin E, while the other group received a placebo. No significant differences in nutritional status between the two groups existed at the start of the study.

After 28 days of supplementation, the group receiving the antioxidant vitamins exhibited significant immune function improvements, including an increase in the absolute number of immune cells (T cells and T4 subsets), T4 to T8 ratio (a measure of immune strength), and immune cell activity. In contrast, the group receiving placebo experienced no improvement in immune functions.

The researchers concluded: "Our results suggest that supplementation with physiological doses of vitamins A, C and E in combination can improve cell-mediated immunity. Further studies are required to see whether such benefits are maintained with long-term vitamin supplementation and whether they are associated with any reduction in morbidity among long-stay patients."

Penn, N.D., et al. The effect of dietary supplementation with vitamins A, C and E on cell-mediated immune function in elderly long-stay patients: a randomized controlled trial. *Age and Ageing.* 1991; 20:169-174.

Antioxidants Enhance Immunity in Healthy Elderly

Thirty-four healthy adults 60 years of age or older resided in a nutrition research unit at Tufts University for 30 days. They were given either 800 IU vitamin E or a placebo each day, along with a carefully controlled diet supplying the U.S. recommended daily allowances of all nutrients.

The results of the study indicated that those who received vitamin E showed an increased level of vitamin E in certain white blood cells, enhanced immune system response, and reduced production of prostaglandin E_2, which inhibits immune responses. Those who received a placebo did not experience these benefits.

The researchers concluded very positively, "It is encouraging to note that a single nutrient can enhance immune responsiveness in healthy elderly subjects consuming the recommended amounts of all nutrients. This is especially significant because dietary intervention represents the most practical approach for delaying or reversing the rate of decline of immune function with age."

Meydani, S.N., et al. Vitamin E supplementation enhances cell-mediated immunity in healthy elderly subjects. *American Journal of Clinical Nutrition*. 1990; 52:557-563.

Antioxidants and Lifespan in Mammals

In a series of studies, researchers measured the level of various antioxidants (carotenes, vitamin E, vitamin C, superoxide dismutase) in several species of mammals. An interesting relationship was observed: the higher the level of antioxidants in a particular species of mammals, the longer was the expected lifespan for that species. For instance, humans had the highest levels of antioxidants, as well as the longest lifespan of all mammals. Horses were found to have roughly half the levels of antioxidants of humans, and their expected lifespan is about half that of humans. Mice and rats had the lowest levels of antioxidants, and also have the shortest expected lifespans.

The results suggest that free radicals play an important role in the process of aging and that sufficient levels of antioxidants are required to prevent premature aging and diseases related to aging. In short, the better an animal is able to fight free radicals, the longer its life expectancy.

The researchers conclude, "The antioxidant status of an individual could be important in determining frequency of age-dependent diseases and duration of general health maintenance."

Cutler, R.G. Antioxidants and aging. *American Journal of Clinical Nutrition*. 1991; 53:373S-379S.

Taking Antioxidants Reduces Risk of
Coronary Heart Disease

The Harvard School of Public Health recently completed the Nurses Health Study and the Health Professionals Follow-up Study, which followed 87,245 U.S. female nurses for 8 years and 45,720 male health professionals for 4 years. In both groups, those who took the highest amounts of vitamin E experienced a statistically significant 32% to 34% reduction in risk for coronary heart disease. Moreover, vitamin supplements were identified to be the primary sources of vitamin E intake.

The study showed several interesting points:

• Vitamin E's protective effect was found in those using supplements of 100 IU or more daily.

• Those whose intake of vitamin E came solely from food did not experience the protective effect.

• The protective effect was enjoyed by those who took vitamin E for two or more years.

Stampfer, M.J., et al. Vitamin E consumption and the risk of coronary disease in women. *New England Journal of Medicine*. 1993; 328:1444-1449.

Rimm, E.B., et al. Vitamin E consumption and the risk of coronary heart disease in men. *New England Journal of Medicine*. 1993; 328:1450-1456.

Antioxidants vs. Heart Disease Death

A World Health Organization study of middle-aged men from 16 European study populations found low blood levels of vitamin E to be the *main risk factor* for death from ischemic heart disease, more than high blood pressure and high cholesterol levels, the traditional risk factors. Quote: "The cross-cultural differences of ischemic heart disease mortality are primarily attributable to plasma status of vitamin E, which might have protective functions."

Gey, K., et al. Inverse correlation between plasma vitamin E and mortality from ischemic heart disease in cross-cultural epidemiology. *American Journal of Clinical Nutrition.* 1991; 53:326S-334S.

Antioxidants vs. Angina Pectoris

The relationship between risk of angina pectoris and blood levels of vitamins A, C, E, and carotene was studied in 504 men. Low levels of vitamins C, E, and carotenes were found to be significant factors in increased risk of angina pectoris, or heart pain. The relationship was especially strong for low levels of vitamin E. The researchers suggest that populations with high coronary heart disease incidence may benefit from diets rich in antioxidants, especially vitamin E.

Riemersma, R.A., et al. Risk of angina pectoris and plasma concentrations of vitamins A, C, and E, and carotene. *Lancet.* 1991; 337:1-5.

Antioxidants vs. Atherosclerosis

Researchers at the Erasmus University Medical School in The Netherlands compared blood levels of vitamin E, selenium, and polyunsaturated fatty acids in patients with atherosclerosis. In all cases, low levels of selenium were found. The ratios of selenium to various polyunsaturated fatty acids were also low, especially in those with low vitamin E levels.

The researchers believe that high blood levels of polyunsaturated fatty acids without sufficient antioxidant protection increase the risk for developing atherosclerosis.

Kok F., et al. Do antioxidants and polyunsaturated fatty acids have a combined association with coronary atherosclerosis? *Atherosclerosis*. 1991; 86:85-90.

Antioxidants Protect Heart During Heart Surgery

During open heart surgery, blood is purposely diverted from the heart to reduce bleeding. When blood flow is restored to the heart, researchers have observed a surge of free-radical production in heart tissue. Heart muscle cells can undergo tremendous structural damage as a result. Antioxidant supplementation before heart surgery can provide effective protection from such free-radical induced damage.

Five days before undergoing coronary artery bypass surgery, 16 patients took 100,000 IU vitamin A and 400 IU vitamin E daily. Another group of patients did not receive any antioxidant supplementation.

Researchers took biopsy samples of heart tissue before diverting blood away from the heart and after blood flow was restored. The results showed that free-radical processes decreased in samples of those who took antioxidants, but increased in samples of those who did not take antioxidants.

The evidence strongly suggests that antioxidant vitamins A and E effectively reduce free-radical processes in heart cells of patients needing open heart surgery, thus protecting the heart during such trauma.

Ferreira, R.F., et al. Antioxidant action of vitamins A and E in patients submitted to coronary artery bypass surgery. *Vascular Surgery.* 1991; 25:191-195.

Antioxidants Reduce Platelet Stickiness

Platelets are cells in the blood responsible for clotting. Without them, a minor cut or bruise would result in massive bleeding and rapid death. However, if platelets become too sticky and clot abnormally inside healthy blood vessels, the clots can obstruct blood flow, starving body tissues of oxygen and food. If those tissues are in the heart, heart disease may result. If they are in the brain, strokes may occur.

In theory, a deficiency of antioxidants may cause platelets in the blood to stick together (aggregate). Supplementation with antioxidant nutrients was found to reduce platelet stickiness, thus potentially decreasing the risk of such ailments as atherosclerosis, heart disease, and stroke.

In a carefully controlled study, 78 men were randomly assigned to receive either a daily antioxidant supplement (45,000 IU beta carotene, 600 mg vitamin C, 300 IU vitamin E, and 75 mcg selenium) or placebo for 5 months. The results were encouraging: those receiving antioxidants enjoyed significant reduction in platelet stickiness, while those on placebo did not.

The researchers believe that one way antioxidants prevent platelet stickiness is by reducing hormones in the blood that tend to promote stickiness.

Salonen, J.T., et al. Effects of antioxidant supplementation on platelet function: a randomized pair-matched, placebo-controlled, double-blind trial in men with low antioxidant status. *American Journal of Clinical Nutrition.* 1991; 53: 1222-1229.

Treatment of Precancerous Lesions
with Antioxidants

Oral leukoplakia is characterized by white lesions in the mouth, which may develop into cancer. Eighteen patients with oral leukoplakia were evaluated after taking 150,000 IU of beta carotene daily for 9 months. At the end of the study, six subjects (33.3%) enjoyed complete regression of lesions, two (11.1%) had partial regression, and three (16.6%) had minimal regression. However, in six patients (33.3%) the leukoplakia did not improve, and in one (5.5%), it worsened. Those who did not respond favorably were strongly associated with smoking and alcohol habits, which may have canceled the benefits of therapy. Overall, the authors of the study believe that beta carotene is fairly effective in preventing oral leukoplakia from developing into cancer, and more clinical studies are warranted.

Toma, S. et al. Treatment of oral leukoplakia with beta carotene. *Oncology.* 49:77-81, 1992.

High Levels of Antioxidants Reduce
Lung Cancer Risk

A study at the Johns Hopkins School of Hygiene and Public Health involved 99 people who were subsequently found to have lung cancer and 196 healthy controls who were carefully matched. The researchers discovered strong relationships between the level of antioxidants in the blood and the risk of lung cancer.

For instance, persons with very low vitamin E blood levels had 2.5 times higher risk of lung cancer than those with high vitamin E blood levels. Low beta carotene blood levels also significantly increased lung cancer risk.

The researchers conclude, "These data support an association between low levels of serum vitamin E and the risk of any type of lung cancer and between low levels of serum beta carotene and the risk of squamous-cell carcinoma of the lung."

Menkes, M.S., et al. Serum beta carotene, vitamins C and E, selenium, and the risk of lung cancer. *New England Journal of Medicine.* 1986; 315:1250-1254.

Antioxidants for Multiple Sclerosis

Multiple sclerosis patients may be deficient in antioxidant nutrients. In a study conducted at the Institute of Hygiene in Aarhus, Denmark, subjects with multiple sclerosis received antioxidant supplements containing 6 mg of sodium selenite, 2000 mg of vitamin C, and 480 mg of vitamin E.

After 5 weeks, the levels of a vital antioxidant enzyme, glutathione peroxidase, increased fivefold. This increase allowed body tissues and muscles to better handle degenerative factors, including free radicals, which affect muscle and nerve function.

The researchers conclude that those with multiple sclerosis are deficient in antioxidant enzymes and nutrients, but respond favorably to antioxidant supplementation.

Mai, J., et al. High dose antioxidant supplementation to MS patients. *Biological Trace Element Research.* 1990; 24: 109.

Antioxidants Help Prevent Cataracts

One hundred seventy-five cataract patients were individually matched with 175 cataract-free subjects in a study at the University of Western Ontario. Everyone in the study filled out a questionnaire on vitamin supplement intake. Investigators analyzed the results and discovered that the cataract-free group consumed more vitamin E and vitamin C than did the cataract group. This study demonstrated that those who took antioxidant supplements enjoyed a 50% reduction in cataract incidence.

Another study confirmed that antioxidants may help prevent cataracts. Researchers at the USDA Human Nutrition Research Center on Aging at Tufts University measured blood antioxidant levels in cataract patients and found these patients to be particularly low in beta carotene, vitamin C, and vitamin E. Moreover, those who ate less than 3.5 servings of fruits and vegetables (which are naturally rich in antioxidant nutrients) per day had an increased risk of cataracts.

These studies support the theory that free-radical damage in the eye plays a major role in cataract formation. Antioxidant supplementation may stop this process from beginning and continuing.

Robertson, J.M., et al. A possible role for vitamins C and E in cataract prevention. *American Journal of Clinical Nutrition*. 1991; 53:346S-351S.

Jacques P.F., et al. Epidemiologic evidence of a role for the antioxidant vitamins and carotenoids in cataract prevention. *American Journal of Clinical Nutrition*. 1991; 53:352S-355S.

Antioxidants Delay Progression of
Parkinson's Disease

Parkinson's disease is a neurological disorder characterized by tremor, rigidity, and loss of movement and reflexes. Although the cause is unknown, a group of medical scientists suggest that brain cells produce excessive toxins, including free radicals, which damage the cells. Thus, the progression of Parkinson's disease may be slowed with antioxidant supplementation.

Researchers at Columbia University College of Physicians and Surgeons and the Neurological Institute of New York gave one group of patients with early Parkinson's disease 3200 IU of vitamin E and 3000 mg of vitamin C per day. These patients avoided traditional medication 2.5 years longer than those who were not given antioxidant supplements.

The results suggest that high doses of antioxidant vitamins C and E slow the progression of the disease, possibly by preventing the buildup of free radicals and other toxins that damage nerve cells.

Fahn, S. An open trial of high-dosage antioxidants in early Parkinson's disease. *American Journal of Clinical Nutrition.* 1991 53:380S-382S.

Beyond Free Radicals

Lest anyone start a crusade against free radicals, recall their importance in producing energy and hormones, fighting infectious agents, and regulating important enzymes in the body. They are not "evil." On the contrary, without them, life would be impossible. Only when free radicals become excessive and uncontrolled can they potentially damage the body.

The antioxidants are vital defenders against excessive free-radical attack. The role of proper nutrition in preventing disease is becoming clearer. Once dismissed by medical authorities as minor players in maintaining health, vitamins and minerals are beginning to be used to treat a wide variety of serious ailments. As the role of antioxidants in combating free-radical damage becomes clearer, we will hopefully be able to learn how to effectively treat diseases which have plagued us for ages.

A revolution in the concept of treating disease may soon occur. Some have already named it the "Nutriceutical Revolution," because it will help displace the dependence upon toxic drugs in treating disease. Instead, physicians will turn to natural, safe substances, such as the nutrients beta carotene, vitamin C, vitamin E, selenium, and other wholesome substances. Already, the revolution seems to have begun, thanks to the growing body of objective scientific evidence to substantiate the effectiveness of such therapies.

Yet, just as no miracle drug will ever cure all the diseases known to humankind, so no miracle nutrient will. If any lesson should be learned, it is that health depends upon much more than a simple formula. Antioxidant supplementation may help to provide many healthy benefits, but it will never replace health-supportive diets and lifestyles.

Finally, the free radical theory of disease, though taking into account much current scientific evidence, is only one theory which tries to explain the nature of disease. It is a good theory but may be replaced by better theories in the future. Nutritional science, like all other sciences, is ever growing and seeking better ways to describe the complicated and even miraculous processes of life. This is certainly a worthy goal, which demands resources, patience, and hard work. The benefits may far outweigh the costs, though, as we are beginning to realize with the use of antioxidants.

Appendix A

In More Detail

(1) A good cell molecule is affected by body processes or environmental factors and becomes (2) a free radical. This reacts with (3) oxygen to form (4) a peroxidized free radical, which attacks (5) another good cell molecule. The results are (6) a damaged cell molecule and (7) another free radical. The new free radical begins the process again unless (8) an antioxidant is present to restore the free radical back into (9) a good cell molecule. The antioxidant becomes (10) deactivated and is either excreted, or in certain cases, reactivated.

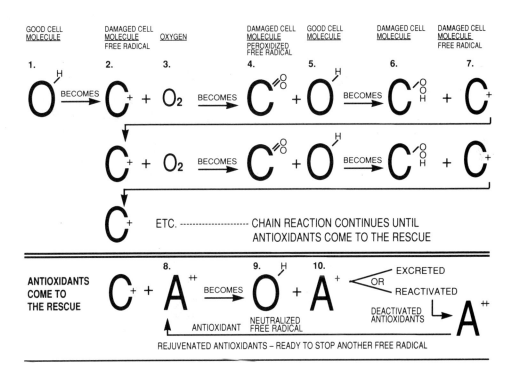

Appendix B

Damage Caused by Free Radicals

Free Radical	Sources	Damage
Superoxide	Body's natural processes	Red blood cell damage Lung damage Degradation of synovial fluid, possibly leading to arthritis
Hydroxyl radical	Radiation body processes	Genetic mutation Cell membrane destruction
Nitrogen dioxide	Cigarette smoke Vehicle exhaust	Irreversible lung damage Cell membrane destruction
Chloroform radical	Chloroform	Liver damage Cell membrane destruction
Quione radicals	Cigarette tar	Genetic mutation Chemical cancer inducer
Bipyridyl radicals	Herbicides	Inhibits biochemical processes Cataract formation

Appendix C

Major Antioxidant Nutrients
Used Clinically

Antioxidant	Principal Roles	Typical Dosages
Beta carotene (provitamin A)	Quenches singlet oxygen Scavenges free radicals Reduces cancer risk	10,000-50,000 IU
Vitamin C (ascorbic acid)	Works in bloodstream and other watery areas Regenerates vitamin E Enhances immune system Antibacterial Antiviral	250-2000 mg
Vitamin E (alpha tocopherol)	Protects cell membrane Works in blood Protects vitamin A and selenium Protects from smog and smoke	200-800 IU
Selenium	Essential part of glutathione peroxidase Acts in concert with vitamin E Protects against cancer	50-200 mcg

Bibliography

An Introduction to Free Radicals. Vitamin Information Service. Vol. 1 No. 2. 1988.

Anti-oxidants: Vitamins A, C, E, and the Mineral Selenium and Free Radicals. Del Mar, CA.: Health Media of America, 1983.

Bendich, A. The Safety of Beta Carotene. *Nutrition and Cancer.* 11:207–214, 1988.

Brock, T.D. and Madigan, M.T. *Biology of Microorganisms,* fifth edition. Englewood Cliffs, New Jersey: Prentice-Hall, 1988.

Burton, G.W. and Ingold, K.U. Beta carotene: An unusual type of lipid antioxidant. *Science* 224:569–573, 1984.

Cheraskin, E.; Ringsdorf, W.M.; and Sisley, E.L. *The Vitamin C Connection.* New York: Harper and Row, 1983.

Erdman, J.W.; Poor, C.L.; and Dietz, J.M. Factors affecting the bioavailability of vitamin A, carotenoids, and vitamin E. *Food Technology* October 1988, p. 214–21.

Erdman, J.W. The physiologic chemistry of carotenes in man. *Clinical Nutrition* 7 (3): 101–106, 1988.

Guyton, A.C. *Human Physiology and Mechanisms of Disease;* fourth edition. Philadelphia: W.B. Saunders, 1987.

Krinsky, N.I. *Antioxidant Functions of Beta Carotene.* Vitamin Nutrition Information Service, Vol. 1 No. 5.

Lachance, P. Dietary intake of carotenes and the carotene gap. *Clinical Nutrition* 7 (3): 118–122, 1988.

Molecular Interrelations of Nutrition and Cancer. Editors: M.S. Arnott, J. van Eys, Y.M. Wang. New York: Raven Press, 1982.

Pryor, W.A. Free radicals in biological systems. *Scientific American* 223 (2): 70–83, 1970.

Pryor, W.A. Free radical pathology. *Chemical & Engineering News* 49: 35–41, 1971.

Roitt, I.M.; Brostoff, J.; and Male, D.K. *Immunology.* London: Gower Medical Publishing Ltd, 1985.

Selenium in biology and medicine. Proceedings of the Third International Symposium on Selenium in Biology and Medicine. New York: Van Nostrand Reinhold, 1984.

Shute, E. *The Heart and Vitamin E.* New Canaan, Conn: Keats Publishing, Inc., 1977.

The American Journal of Clinical Nutrition. Antioxidant supplement to Volume 53, January 1991.

Third Conference on Vitamin C. *Annals of the New York Academy of Sciences,* Vol. 498, 1987.

Vitamin E: A Comprehensive Treatise. Basic and Clinical Nutrition, Volume 1. Editor: Lawrence J. Machlin. New York: Marcel Dekker, Inc., 1980.

Vitamin E: Biochemistry and Health Implications. *Annals of the New York Academy of Sciences,* Vol. 570, 1989.

Vitamin E: Biochemical, Hematological, and Clinical Aspects. *Annals of the New York Academy of Sciences,* Vol. 393, 1982.

Vitamin E and Other Antioxidants: Weapons Against Cancer. Vitamin E Update. Fine Chemical Division of Henkel Corporation. Vol. 1 No. 1, March 1989.

Wolf, G. Is dietary beta carotene an anti-cancer agent? *Nutrition Reviews* 40 (9): 257–60, 1982.